Male

Female

Two mallards on
the bank of a river

A flock of wild
geese flying south
in a V shape

Barn owl's big
wings make no
sound as they flap.

Wing feathers
are almost
fully grown.

Baby blue tits
in a tree nest

Barn owl
coming in
to land

Young bird
explorer
looks at birds
in the sky.

Birds

Written by
JILL BAILEY and DAVID BURNIE

Stoddart

A DORLING KINDERSLEY BOOK

Senior editor Susan McKeever **Art editor** Vicky Wharton
Editor Jodi Block **Senior art editor** Jacquie Gulliver
Production Catherine Semark
Editorial consultant Peter Colston, The British Museum
(Natural History), Tring.

Published in Canada in 1992 by Stoddart Publishing Co. Limited
34 Lesmill Road
Toronto, Canada M3B 2T6

Published in Great Britain in 1992 by Dorling Kindersley Limited
9 Henrietta Street Covent Garden
London WC2E 8PS
England
Reprinted 1995

Canadian Cataloguing in Publication Data
Bailey, Jill
Birds

(Eyewitness explorers)
ISBN 0-7737-2578-4

1. Birds – Juvenile literature. 2. Birds – Identification – Juvenile literature. I. Burnie, David.
II. Title. III. Series.

QL676.2.B35 1992   j598   C92-093054-9

Color reproduction by Colourscan, Singapore
Printed by A. Mondadori Editore, Verona

Contents

8. Looking at birds

10. What is a bird?

12. Feathered friends

14. Taking to the air

16. Patterns in the air

18. From soaring to bounding

20. Finding a mate

22. Eggs and hatching

24. The first days

26. The first flight

28. Good parents

30. Cup-shaped nests

32. Strange nests

34. Cleaning and preening

36. Feeding habits

38. Meat-eating birds

40. Night hunters

42. Bird territories

44. Flying away

46. Birds of the sea

48. Birds of the shore

50. Freshwater birds

52. Woodland birds

54. Desert and grassland birds

56. Tropical birds

58. City birds

60. Index

Looking at birds

You may not always notice birds, but they are all over the place – in the garden, by the seashore, in the city. If you become a bird-watcher, soon you will begin to notice all sorts of things about birds – how they feed, how they fly, and the different sounds that they make.

Keep quiet!
No bird likes noise and bustle. So be as quiet as you can when watching birds.

Gray crown

Brown feathers on back

Black bib

House sparrow
This sassy bird is a common sight in gardens and cities. You can recognize it by its brown back, gray crown, and black bib.

Choose a lightweight pair of binoculars for looking at birds close up.

Dressed for the part
When watching birds, wear dull colors so that you don't stand out too much from the background. Make sure you have some warm, water-proof clothing in case it gets cold or wet.

This is a male sparrow. Females are almost entirely brown.

How to draw a bird

The best way to remember a bird you see is to draw it.
It is easier than you think to draw a bird. Build up your
sketch from simple shapes.

1 Draw
two circles –
one for the
head and one for the
body. Leave a space
between the circles.

2 Add the neck,
beak, legs, and tail.

3 Fill in the pattern
of the feathers.

1 Use a
half circle
for the
body of a
water bird.

1 When
drawing a
bird in flight, start
with two circles.

2 Add the
outstretched
wings, tail, neck, and
beak. Is the head held
out or tucked in?

3 Add the
wing details.

Hat

Waterproof
coat

*The best kind of
notebook to use is a
spiral-bound one with
a stiff back. Jot down
the shape of the bird
you see, its color, and
the way it flies.*

What is a bird?

Birds come in many shapes and sizes, but there are some things that unite all birds. All of them are covered with feathers for warmth. They all have two wings, although not all birds can fly. Their legs and feet are covered by small scales, and most have only four toes. All birds have beaks, and they all lay eggs.

Long, sharp beaks are good for finding food in the soil or vegetation.

Birds have many feathers.

Legs and feet are covered by scaly skin.

Spotting starlings
There are about 9,000 species of birds, and each one has its own special features. You can recognize a starling by its shiny black feathers with a purple or green sheen. In winter, its feathers are speckled white.

Bird beaks
Birds have no hands, so they use their beaks to pick up or tear up food. Different beaks are suited to eating different foods.

Goshawks are meat-eaters. They have very hooked beaks for tearing apart flesh.

Many ducks feed by dabbling. They open and shut their beaks to take in water. Then they strain out food.

The green-finch is a seed-eater, so its short, thick bill is strong enough to crack open hard seeds.

A bird's hollow, lightweight beak is made of horny material. It is very strong. Birds use their beaks to feed, preen, and build their nests.

Ancient wing

The oldest fossil bird, called *Archaeopteryx*, which means "ancient wing," lived 150 million years ago among the dinosaurs. This creature was part bird, part reptile. It was covered with feathers, like all birds, but it also had jaws with very small teeth and claw-like fingers on its wings, like reptiles.

The starling has a big keel, or breastbone. The powerful muscles that make the wings beat are attached to this bone.

Underneath its skin

Here is a starling without its skin! You have lots of bones under your skin too. But a bird's bones contain many air spaces. These make the bones light for flying. A bird has very long legs – so what look like its knees are really its ankles.

Ankle

Perching birds have one toe that points backward to grasp branches.

Fancy footwork

Birds may use their feet for perching in trees, running across the ground, or swimming. Some birds use their feet to catch prey.

Many birds that live in lakes and rivers have webbed feet for paddling.

The feet of birds of prey have long claws for gripping their victims.

11

Feathered friends

Birds are the only animals with feathers. A large bird, such as a swan, may have more than 25,000 feathers, and even a tiny hummingbird has almost 1,000. Feathers keep birds warm and dry and allow them to fly. They are very light, which makes it easy for birds to stay in the air. A bird's feathers come in many beautiful colors and shapes.

The alula prevents stalling in flight. The kestrel's unusually large alula lets it fly well at low speeds.

Coverts make a smooth surface for air to flow over.

Primary feathers provide the main power for flying.

Secondary feathers are curved to make air flow up under the wing, lifting the bird.

Kestrel wing
Here are some feathers that make up a kestrel's wing. You can see the wing in action on the right. Feathers are made of hollow rods called quills. Branches on either side in turn have smaller branches linked together by tiny hooks too small to see.

Coverts also help give the wing a curved shape to provide lift.

Soft fringes on the edges of an owl's feathers muffle any noise made by the wings in flight as the owl approaches a mouse.

The down at the base of a buzzard's coverts keep it warm.

Finding feathers

Start collecting any feathers that you find along the roadside, on the beach, or in the woods. Fix them to paper with tape or put them in clear plastic holders. Make notes about where and when you found them, and label as many as possible.

Hanging out to dry

A cormorant squeezes the air out of its feathers so it can dive and travel around underwater more easily, in search of fish. Afterward, it spends a long time with its wings spread, drying them out.

As the kestrel beats its wings down, it spreads its feathers out to press against the air.

Feather forms

A kestrel uses its long wing and tail feathers for flying. But like all birds, it has feathers that are not used for flight. Smaller feathers cover the rest of the body, making it waterproof and windproof. Fluffy down feathers underneath keep the bird warm.

Tail feathers act as a rudder for steering. They can also be lowered and spread out to act as a brake.

Taking to the air

A bird stays in the air by flapping its wings. As it pulls its wings down, the feathers push against the air, moving the bird up and forward.

The feathers twist to let air through as the wings rise.

The wings of this pigeon are as high as they can go, and the feathers are spread apart.

Flying like a plane

Some birds can also fly like airplanes, using the force of the air to keep them in flight. This type of flight uses much less energy because the birds rarely flap their wings. As air flows faster over the curved surface of a wing and slower underneath, it creates a force that pushes the bird up. This upward force is called lift.

The owl's broad wings allow it to fly slowly but still stay in the air.

With a few powerful flaps, it is airborne.

Silent flight

Compared to the pigeon, the barn owl has broad wings and a slow, silent flight. It flaps its way over fields and hedges, watching and listening for small animals. Because it is so quiet, it can swoop onto prey without giving itself away.

The owl springs into the air with a kick of its feet.

Fast fliers

Pigeons are powerful and speedy fliers. They are good at taking off in a hurry and can fly for many hours without a break. Some pigeons are specially trained for racing. You can recognize racing pigeons because they often have rings around their legs, showing who they belong to.

The feathers start to flick upward, ready for the next beat of the wings.

As the pigeon pulls its wings downward, the feathers flatten out to make a single surface.

The feathers separate as the wings begin to rise again.

Happy landing

Landing safely is an important part of flying. The bird has to slow down at just the right time so that it drops gently to the ground. Young birds have to practice before they can land properly.

When the owl spots a mouse, it starts to drop and swings its legs down.

Near the ground, the owl uses its wings as brakes.

Patterns in the air

When you see a bird in flight, notice the pattern it makes. Different kinds of birds fly in different ways. Large, heavy birds such as ducks flap their wings all the time. Many smaller birds save their energy by gliding between flaps. Some birds hover in the air as they search for prey or feed at flowers.

Drawing flight patterns

Quick sketches of a bird's flight can help to identify the bird, even if it is a long way off. Draw an outline of the shape the bird makes in flight, and then show the way it flies with arrows.

The fulmar's long, narrow wings help it to glide.

Look for birds gliding near sea cliffs.

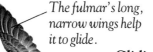

Gliding

The fulmar soars upward on the rising air currents that form when the wind blowing from the sea meets the cliffs. Then it glides slowly down across the sea. It can travel a long way without flapping its wings at all.

Hovering

The kestrel beats its wings forward and spreads its tail feathers in order to hover. Doing this, it can spot mice on the ground below. Look for kestrels hovering over grassy strips bordering roads.

Tail fanned out for balance

The mallard duck sticks its neck out when it flies.

Large wings and powerful flight muscles lift the heavy body.

Straight line

Ducks and geese often fly in a V formation or in straight lines, beating their wings all the time.

If you spot a mallard flying over open ground, it is probably on its way to a lake or a river.

Kestrels like to hover over roads, where they can spot prey at the roadsides.

From soaring to bounding

Meat-eating birds often need to fly long distances in search of a meal. To save energy, they soar on air currents. Many smaller birds do not need to fly so far. Some keep close to hedges and trees, where their enemies will not spot them.

Soaring birds have long, broad wings with finger-like tips.

Stooping

The peregrine falcon swoops down on other smaller birds in a vertical dive known as a stoop. Spot the sky diver near mountains or cliffs.

Tail is fanned out.

Soaring

Eagles soar on thermals – warm pockets of rising air – so they don't have to flap their wings much. In this way, they can keep an eye on the ground and save energy as well!

The martial eagle soars high in the sky, so you have to look through binoculars to see it!

Where do they soar?

Soaring birds go where the thermals are – over mountains and wide open plains.

If you want to spot a hummingbird, look for a tiny bird, as small as your finger, and listen for a whirring sound – this is its wings beating.

Flying backward

The hummingbird is the only bird that can fly sideways, forward, and backward. It is also the best hoverer of all. It needs to hover to feed on nectar from flowers.

Hummingbirds hover in front of flowers as they sip the sweet nectar.

The nectar in the flower gives the hummingbird the energy to hover.

Bounding

Bluetits and many other small birds have a slightly bounding flight. They flap their wings in short bursts, and then rest and glide. This saves energy.

Although this flight pattern is slightly exaggerated, small birds look as if they are bouncing up and down on the end of an elastic band!

Bluetits close their wings in between bursts of flapping.

Finding a mate

Before it can breed, a bird has to find a partner. Courtship is the way of attracting a mate that is of the right age and sex, and, most important, of the same type. Usually, the male attracts the female. If she is impressed by his courtship behavior or his bright colors, she will mate with him and lay eggs.

Friend or foe?

These Sandwich terns look as though they are fighting over a fish. But they are courting. The male offers his partner the fish as a gift. The two birds then fly off together.

Bird bonding

Once the terns have landed, the female must accept the fish from the male one last time. This shows that she is willing to pair up. Many male birds give their partners food when they are courting. This helps to make a bond between the pair.

The male has a pouch of stretchy skin on the front of his throat.

Great frigate bird

Frigate birds spend most of their lives flying high up over the sea. They nest on tropical islands. Each male bird picks a site for the nest and then attracts a mate by blowing up his special pouch.

A frigate bird's wings are wider than the height of a man.

Hanging around

The male bluebird of paradise attracts his mate by opening his wings and tipping forward until he is hanging upside down by his feet. You may not spot this bird flying around your back garden, but you might see one in the zoo.

When the male hangs upside down, his dazzling blue feathers open up like a fan.

Red balloon

To attract a female, the male frigate bird blows up his pouch like a balloon. When she comes near, he rattles his beak against the pouch and flaps his wings.

A frigate bird can keep his pouch blown up for some time.

Eggs and hatching

A bird's egg is a living package protected by a hard shell. When it is newly laid, the egg contains just the yolk and the white part. The parent keeps the egg warm by sitting on it, or "incubating" it. The yolk nourishes the growing bird, and after a few weeks, the bird is ready to hatch.

Ground nester
The curlew nests on the ground. Its speckled eggs are well camouflaged.

Blue egg
The American robin lays four blue eggs.

Pea-sized eggs
A hummingbird's nest has enough room for two pea-sized eggs.

Eagles lay two eggs. One hatches a few days before the other.

One of a kind
Many guillemot eggs have spots or streaks. Parents can recognize their own egg by its unique pattern.

Jungle giant
The cassowary is a big flightless bird. The female lays up to six eggs, but you will not often see eggs of this size.

Cuckoos lay their big eggs in other birds' nests. Redstart "foster parents" cannot tell the difference. Can you?

Into the outside world

If you tap an egg with a spoon, its shell will quickly break. But imagine how hard the same job is for a baby bird. It has to break the shell from the inside. It has a special eggtooth on the top of its bill, so it can chip through the shell. Here you can see how a duckling breaks out.

1 Making a hole
The duckling's hardest task comes first. Using its beak, it chips away at the blunt end of the egg until it has made a hole.

2 Round and round
Next, the duckling hammers away at the shell. It turns all the time, so that it cuts in a circle.

3 Pushing away
Once the circle is complete, the duckling gives a big heave by trying to straighten its neck. As the crack widens, one of its wings pops out.

🖐 *Remember – never touch birds' eggs in the wild.*

4 Off with the top
Suddenly, the blunt end of the egg breaks open as the duckling gives a final push. It is almost into the outside world.

5 Breaking out
The duckling falls out of the egg, landing on its stomach. Its wet feathers cling together, making it look bedraggled.

6 Drying off
Within two or three hours, the duckling's feathers have dried out and turned fluffy. It cannot fly yet, but it can run around and is ready for its first swim.

The first days

A duckling can feed itself when it is just a day old. But not all birds are like this. Many are blind and helpless when they hatch, and they rely on their parents to bring food to them. For adult blue tits, this means many days of hard work.

Eyes not yet fully formed

Feathers on wings

Feathers grow in a line along the back.

2 Growing feathers
By the time the young birds are six days old, their feathers have started to grow.

Open wide
Many baby birds have special colored patterns inside their mouths. These show the parents where to put food.

1 The new family
These baby blue tits are just four days old. They are blind and bald, and hardly look like birds at all. When one of their parents arrives at the nest with food, they open their beaks wide and stretch upward.

Wing feathers are
protected by
waxy tubes.

Eyes are
beginning
to open.

Tips of wing
feathers beginning
to appear

3 Fast food
The baby birds are now nine days old.
Their parents bring them food almost
once a minute, and so the nestlings
quickly gain weight.

4 Growing up
Thirteen days after hatching, the
nestlings are starting to look like
their parents. Within the next
week, their wing and tail
feathers will be fully
grown, and they will
be ready to fly.

Eyes fully open

Short on space
By the time they are ready to fly,
many young birds are heavier than
their parents. They are so big that
they can hardly fit in the nest.

25

The first flight

Baby birds know how to fly naturally,
so they do not have to learn to fly.
But they do need to practice in
order to learn how to twist and turn
in the air and how to land without
falling on their faces.

*The bird's flight
feathers are not
fully grown.*

*A baby chaffinch
nervously makes
its first flight, as its
parents call out to
encourage it.*

Follow the leader

At first, baby chaffinches stay safely
hidden among the branches near their nest.
After a few days, they can fly quite well. Then the
young birds follow their parents around as they hunt
for food. This saves the parents time and energy, as
they no longer have to carry food back to the nest.

Brave babies

Little Auks nest on cliff ledges high above the sea, where most of their enemies cannot reach them. On their very first flight, the baby auks must reach the sea below. There they will learn how to catch fish to eat. If they don't reach the sea, they will crash-land on the rocks.

Look out below!

The wood duck lays her eggs in a tree hole up to 50 feet above the ground, out of reach of foxes and other enemies. Before the ducklings are a day old, they must leap out of the tree. Their mother waits on the ground below, calling to them to follow her. When they have all landed safely, she will lead them to water and food.

Before landing, the baby chaffinch lowers its wing and tail feathers to slow down, then lowers its legs to absorb the shock as it hits the ground.

Wood ducklings spread their tiny wings and feet to slow their fall. Amazingly, they usually manage to land without getting hurt.

Good parents

Most new parents have to work very hard when a baby arrives, and birds are no exception. Newborn birds are usually helpless, so their parents have to feed them, keep them clean, and guard them from other animals that may want to eat them. Most parent birds tuck the chicks under their feathers to keep them warm or to shade them from the hot sun.

Egg impostor
Cuckoo parents avoid looking after their young by laying their eggs in other birds' nests. When the baby cuckoo hatches, it pushes the others out of the nest. This cuckoo is bigger than its foster parents, but they continue to feed it.

Penguin parents
Penguins come ashore to rear their chicks. But they need to travel far out to sea to hunt for fish. The parents take turns looking after the chick. One parent stays with the chick while the other goes out to sea to fish.

The penguin chick has a thick, fluffy coat, but it still huddles against its parent to keep warm.

Penguin parents look after their chicks until they grow a coat of stiff, waterproof feathers.

Light as a feather

Swans lay their eggs in a big nest on the riverbank. Baby swans can swim and find their own food soon after they hatch. They are so light that they float easily on the water. Every day their parents lead them to safe places to feed. Swans can be very fierce when they are guarding their young. They will attack any animal that comes too close, even humans – so be careful if you see them.

Baby swans are called cygnets. These cygnets are enjoying a ride on their mother's back, safe and warm among her feathers. The father swan has raised his wings so he looks big and frightening.

Reaching for a fish

A pelican chick reaches far inside its parent's throat in search of food. The parent pelican flies out to sea and catches lots of fish. It swallows them all and flies home. Then it coughs up the fish for the chick to eat.

The herring gull chick is not as brightly colored as its parents. This helps it to hide from foxes, bigger gulls, and other enemies.

Parent peckers

A hungry herring gull chick pecks at the bright red spot at the tip of its parent's bill. This persuades its parent to cough up food. The hungry chick gobbles it up.

29

Cup-shaped nests

A bird's nest is its home – this is where it lays its eggs and raises its young. The nest helps to keep the eggs and baby birds sheltered and warm. Many birds build cup-shaped nests high above the ground in trees.

Hard work
The female chaffinch has to make several hundred trips to collect all the right materials in order to build her nest.

The chaffinch decorates the outside of its nest with lichen, which makes it hard to find.

Turning around slowly in the nest and using its breast for pushing, the chaffinch makes the cup shape.

Chaffinch nest
The chaffinch builds its nest in a small fork in a bush or tree. The nest is made of grass, moss, and roots, and is lined with feathers and hairs to keep the eggs warm.

A hard bed

Instead of a downy bed, baby song thrushes have to sleep on a hard bed of mud. The song thrush makes a cup-shaped nest of roots, hairs, and grass. Finally, it adds a thin lining of mud.

Mud lining is made from wet mud.

Mud becomes hard and strong when it dries.

Mud collector

The female song thrush collects grass, roots, dead leaves, twigs, and wet mud from puddles.

Spot the home maker

If you see a bird carrying grass or twigs, it is probably building a nest. This magpie is on its way to its big nest high in tall hedges.

Wool caught on barbed wire fences makes a warm nest lining.

Pieces of tree bark give a nest strength.

Nest ingredients

Pieces of string, wool, ribbons, human hair, and spiderwebs have all been found woven into birds' nests.

Mud is picked up from puddles and stream banks.

String can be found among household and garden trash.

Twigs and leaves

Strange nests

Not all nests are cup-shaped. Some birds just scrape hollows in the ground. Others use strange materials: Tiny cave swiftlets make little cup-shaped nests of their own saliva, which hardens as it dries on the cave wall. The mallee fowl builds a huge mound of sand and buries its eggs in the middle.

The chicks live in the round part of the nest.

Weaver bird nest
Weavers make their nests by weaving lots of pieces of grass together. Their nests are light and airy but also strong and waterproof. The long "tunnel" leading to the nest stops snakes and other enemies from getting inside to eat the eggs and young.

Entrance to nest

Weaving a home
The male weaver bird starts with a knotted ring hanging from a tree. Then it weaves fresh grass in and out until the nest is completed.

Penduline tit nest

This soft hanging nest was made by a penduline tit, using spiderwebs, moss, and grasses. It has a false entrance to fool predators. The real entrance is a narrow slit just above this "entrance," which closes as soon as the bird has entered or left.

This looks like the entrance, but in fact it leads to a small, empty chamber.

The reed warbler needs to be an acrobat to build its nest.

The penduline tit hovers outside its nest.

Nest chamber is at the bottom.

Reedy nest

The reed warbler makes a nest of fresh grasses, reed flowers, and feathers in a reed bed. As sun dries out the reeds, they turn brown, and so do the grasses that make up the warbler's nest.

Dirty work

Cliff swallows make their nests out of mud pellets. Collecting the mud could be dirty work, so they hold their wings and tails well out of the way.

Nest is well hidden among reeds.

Reeds often blow around in the wind.

Cleaning and preening

Birds must keep their feathers in perfect condition. If they are dirty or ruffled, it is difficult to fly and keep warm, so they need constant care. A good place to watch birds clean their feathers is by a birdbath or a puddle in the park. Afterward, they comb the feathers with their beaks. This is called preening.

Preening time

The starling runs each ruffled feather through its bill to make it smooth. Then it uses its bill to collect oil from a preen gland at the base of its tail. It wipes the oil over its feathers to condition or waterproof them.

The starling uses its bill to zip up the branches, or barbs, of its feathers.

Zipped-up feathers

Unzipped, ruffled feathers

Zipped up

The little branches of the feathers have tiny hooks that can be zipped up to make a smooth, strong surface for flying.

Splish splash

A good splash in the water is the first step in a bird's cleaning routine. Bathing birds fluff up their feathers and then duck down and use their wings to splash water over their bodies.

A bathing starling flicks its bill from side to side in the water.

Make a birdbath

You can make a birdbath from a sheet of plastic and a few stones. Birds need a gentle slope so they can paddle in and out, and a rough surface so they don't slip.

1 Dig a hole about six inches deep and a yard wide. The hole should have gently sloping sides so small birds can easily get in and out.

2 Line the hole with a sheet of tough plastic. Hold the lining down with stones and sprinkle gravel or sand over it.

4 Fill the bath slowly with water. Keep it full and make sure the water does not freeze in winter. Watch the birds bathing all year.

3 Put some stones in the middle and stick a twig in them to make a perch.

Feeding habits

Birds have many different ways of feeding. Swifts catch insects in flight. Starlings push their beaks into the soil to seize grubs. Herons use their bills for spearing fish, while chaffinches use their beaks for cracking seeds.

Tits regularly hang upside down on a feeding bell.

Acrobatic birds

The black-capped chickadee and other tits are the acrobats of the bird world. They hang upside down from twigs as they search for insects.

Tits use their tail feathers to help them balance.

Snail smasher

If you find a heap of broken snail shells in a corner of the garden, you may have discovered a song thrush's anvil. The thrush has a favorite stone on which it smashes open shells to get the snail inside.

Floating umbrella

When the black heron hunts fish, it lowers its head and neck and spreads its wings around until they meet in front. It looks like an umbrella floating on the surface. This shades the water from the sun, making it easier to spot fish.

Feed the birds

A feeding bell on a rope attracts acrobatic tits and nuthatches, and provides a safe feeding place out of reach of cats. To make a feeding bell, you'll need a yogurt container, a piece of strong string, some bird food (seeds, nuts, raisins, crumbs), some melted fat (lard, suet, or grease), and a mixing bowl.

1 Make a small hole in the bottom of the container. Thread the string through and secure it with a large knot or tie a small twig on the end.

2 Ask an adult to warm the fat until it melts. Then mix in the bird food in a bowl.

Meal in a nutshell

The nuthatch wedges an acorn or hazelnut into a crack in tree bark, and then hammers the nut open to reach the seed inside.

3 Spoon the mixture into the cup and leave it in a cool place until it hardens.

4 Hang the bell on a tree in the garden or on the side of a bird table. Watch for tits performing as they feed.

Nuts eaten by birds have jagged holes or are split in two. Nuts left by mice have round holes and teeth marks.

Pinecones split open by crossbills have a ragged look.

Crossed bills

The red crossbill has a unique bill that crosses over at the tips. It is designed to pry seeds out of pinecones, but it can also pick bark off tree trunks to reach insects.

Meat-eating birds

There are many meat-eaters in the bird world. The ones that hunt by swooping and attacking with their claws are called birds of prey. Most birds of prey watch for food from high in the air, so this is the best place to look for them.

Shrikes catch small animals with their beaks. They store their food by spearing it on thorns.

The bald eagle uses its huge, hooked beak for pulling apart the bodies of fish and other animals.

Feathered hunters

Birds of prey are not the only birds that hunt. Many other birds, such as shrikes, also feed by catching very small animals and insects. But they use their beaks, not their claws, to catch food.

Fishing from the air

The majestic bald eagle fishes from the air. It flaps over the water, snatches up a fish in its claws, and then flies away with it to a perch. Bald eagles are usually seen near lakes, rivers, and coasts.

Eyes in the sky

The kestrel is one of the few birds of prey that can hover. By fluttering its wings very quickly, it can hang in the air as it pinpoints its prey. Grassy roadsides are good places to spot kestrels in action.

From its position in the sky, the kestrel can watch for small animals below.

Cleaning up

Vultures may not be very popular birds, but they do a useful job in eating up the remains of dead animals. They peck holes in carcasses and stretch out their long necks to feed inside. One kind of vulture carries bones high into the air and drops them onto rocks to crack them open. Then it feeds on the soft marrow inside.

Vultures soar high in the sky in search of food. They also keep a close watch on one another. When one bird spots a meal, others quickly follow it.

Most vultures have no feathers on their heads, because blood would dirty their feathers when they feed. The king vulture is unusual because its head is brightly colored.

Night hunters

When the sun sets, most birds settle down for the night. But owls are different. Most of them spend the day asleep and wake up when it gets dark. Owls hunt small animals at night by using their sensitive eyes and ears.

The owl's forward-pointing eyes have spotted its prey – can you find it too?

These feathery tufts look like ears. But this owl's real ears are lower down, hidden at the sides of its face.

Pinpointing prey
Owls have "binocular" vision. This means that both their eyes point in the same direction, just like ours. This way of seeing lets an owl know exactly how far away its prey is.

Still life
The long-eared owl spends the day perched motionless on a branch. It is very difficult to see, because its feathers make it look just like a piece of wood. This owl has long "ear" tufts that it can raise or lower. These help it to recognize other owls of the same type, or species.

Sight and sound
Owls can see their prey by moonlight or even by starlight. They can also hunt when it is completely dark. They do this by using their very sensitive hearing.

The barn owl
The barn owl lives all over the world, from America to Australia. Like other owls, it has a flat face. This guides sounds into its ears, which are hidden under its feathers.

The barn owl catches small animals with its claws and carries them off in its beak. It swallows them whole.

These long bones are the legs of a vole.

Each hipbone has a tiny, round hollow where the leg bone fits in.

Jawbones separate into two parts, but it is easy to match them up.

What's on the menu?
After an owl has eaten, it coughs up a pellet. This contains the bones and fur of its prey. Old pellets are quite safe to handle, and you can gently pull them apart with tweezers to see what an owl has been eating.

Finding pellets
The best place to look for pellets is in old barns or around tree trunks. Old matchboxes make good containers for storing the bones.

By counting the skulls in a pellet, you can see how many animals the owl has eaten.

41

Bird territories

The world of birds is full of private property. These pieces of land are called territories. They are an important part of the way many birds live. By claiming a territory, a bird can make sure that it has somewhere to attract a mate, somewhere to nest, and enough space for a growing family.

Jungle showplace
The male cock-of-the-rock has a small territory on the forest floor where he shows off his plumage to females.

A visiting female watches the males as they parade on the ground below.

Star performer
Males display their crests and their feathers. The female will mate with the one who puts on the best performance.

Each male displays on his own area.

Crest

Bird song

To us, bird song is just a pretty sound. But to birds, it is a way of sending messages about their territories.

Robins sing from high perches so that they can be heard a long way off.

It's my garden!

Male European robins often set up territories in gardens. The owner sings loudly to tell other robins where his territory is.

Battling redbreasts

If another male robin flies into the territory, a battle quickly follows.

Keep your distance

Gannets are large seabirds that nest together on rocky cliffs and islands. Around each nest is a small territory, reaching just as far as the bird on the nest can stretch.

The pairs of nesting gannets have to stay beyond the "pecking distance" of their neighbors.

Male gannets use special displays and loud calls to defend their nests.

Flying away

Have you noticed how some birds disappear in winter?
Have you ever wondered where they go? Many live in
two different places.

Wild geese migrate in V-shaped flocks. Flying in this formation uses less energy. Each bird gets a lift from the force of the bird in front.

They spend winter where it is warmer. In spring, they fly away to raise their families where there is plenty of food. These journeys are migrations.

Flight of the snow goose
Snow geese breed in the Arctic tundra and migrate south to the Gulf of Mexico. Their journey is about 2,000 miles long. The world's greatest bird traveler, the Arctic tern, makes a round trip of 25,000 miles!

Shorter days in late summer tell the snow goose that it is time to fly south.

Arctic tundra

Arctic
North America
Gulf of Mexico
South America

Counting the birds

Here is a quick way to count the birds in a migrating flock. Make a circle with your thumb and index finger. Then hold your arm out and count the birds in the circle. See roughly how many circles it takes to cover the whole flock. Multiply the first number by the second to get the answer.

Snow geese use the sun and stars as a compass to help them find their way.

Traveling geese

Snow geese travel in flocks that can contain tens of thousands of birds. They pause on their long journey to rest and feed at their favorite lakes. At night, you can hear the geese calling as they fly overhead.

In Mexico, snow geese eat lots of plants to build strength for their return journey.

Herald of summer

According to an old saying, "one swallow doesn't make a summer." But when swallows arrive, you can be sure that summer is not far behind. In autumn, young swallows migrate with their parents. The following spring, many find their way from southern Africa to Europe by instinct.

Some snow geese are blue-gray instead of white. They are called blue snow geese.

A coded aluminum ring is put on this bird's leg to find out its movements and life span.

Gulf of Mexico

Birds of the sea

Many seabirds make their homes on rocky cliffs where they are safer from their enemies. Each bird has its favorite nesting place. Puffins like grassy slopes at the top of cliffs, while gannets are happy on bare rock. Seabirds often spend the winter months far out at sea and come ashore to breed.

Gannets dive headfirst into the sea to catch fish. They fold their wings back before they hit the water.

Diving gannets
Gannets feed on fish such as mackerel and herring. A gannet has a special shock-absorbing layer under its skin. This protects it when it dives into the water.

Gannet group
Gannets always breed together, in groups of up to 50,000 nests.

The female gannet lays a single egg on a nest made of seaweed.

Long, hooked beak

Pirate ahoy!
The frigate bird can catch fish for itself, but it prefers to steal food from other birds. Frigate birds fly a long way out to sea, but they hardly ever land on the water. If they do, they have trouble taking off again.

Forked tail for steering when chasing other birds

The frigate bird chases other birds in the air and forces them to drop their food.

Short wing

Puffins can hold lots of fish at once in their bills.

Cliff-top clowns
With their large, striped bills and bright orange feet, puffins are hard to miss. They tunnel in soft ground on grassy slopes and islands, and catch fish out at sea.

Webbed feet spread out for landing.

Long, pointed wing

Puffins use old rabbit burrows or dig burrows for themselves using their bills.

The guillemot's egg is pear-shaped, so that it rolls around in a circle instead of falling off the cliff.

Perched on the edge
The guillemot (*gill-i-mot*) makes no nest at all but lays its single egg on a cliff ledge. The parent bird holds the egg in its feet. Guillemots nest in big, noisy colonies.

Birds of the shore

Sandy beaches are fine for swimming and sunbathing. But if you want to watch shore birds, the thing to look for is lots of sticky mud. Muddy shores contain a hidden world of small animals, from worms to tiny snails, and many different kinds of birds feed on them. Most of these birds are waders – birds with long legs and probing beaks.

Beak with a bend
You don't have to be the world's smartest bird-watcher to recognize an avocet, because it is one of the few birds with a beak that curves upward.

Although it can swim, the avocet usually strides through the water on its long legs. Its legs are so long that they trail behind the avocet when it flies.

The avocet moves its beak from side to side in the water, snapping it shut when it feels food.

A feast in the mud
The bar-tailed godwit reaches deep into the mud with its long beak, which snaps open and shut just like a pair of tweezers.

Strong, orange bill

The stone turner

Flocks of turnstones can be seen walking along the shore in search of food. These small birds turn over stones with their probing bills, hoping to find crabs and other small animals.

Shell smasher

If you have ever collected seashells, you know how tough they are. But small shells are no match for the oystercatcher. With sharp blows of its strong, rod-like beak, it smashes them open and eats the soft animals inside.

The herring gull uses its powerful beak to pull apart its food and also to peck its way to the front in the scramble to eat.

Anything goes

Some birds are very choosy about what they eat, but the herring gull will feed on almost anything. Dead fish, baby birds, earthworms, and rotting garbage are all on the menu when it looks for food.

Freshwater birds

Ponds, streams, rivers, and lakes are often teeming with small animals and plants. These living things – fish, young insects, shrimps, and waterweed – are all food for freshwater birds. Most of these birds feed by swimming on the surface or diving. Others wade through the shallows. But the kingfisher catches small fish by diving at them from a perch.

Drake

Duck

Mallard mixture
Mallards live near ponds, lakes, and streams. The male (called the drake) has a shiny green head. The female (called the duck) is drab and brown.

Tail in the air
Mallards feed in two ways. They either upend to reach food just below the surface, or they scoop small animals and plants off the surface.

You can recognize a kingfisher by its bright turquoise feathers.

The kingfisher hits its prey against a perch to stun it, and then swallows it headfirst.

Attack from the air

The best place to see a kingfisher is from a bridge. Here you can watch it darting up and down a stream or river. The kingfisher spells danger to small fish. It plunges in headfirst, catches a fish in its beak, and then flies to a perch to eat it.

Kingfishers make nests in riverbank burrows. They peck away at the earth, and then kick out the pieces.

The spoonbill's special diet makes its feathers pink.

The spoonbill dips its beak into the water and waves it from side to side.

A beak with two spoons

It is easy to see how the spoonbill gets its name. The ends of the beak are broad and round, just like a pair of spoons. The spoonbill wades slowly through the water with its beak half-open. When it feels food, its two "spoons" snap together.

With its long legs, the spoonbill can wade into deep water.

Woodland birds

Woods are home to hundreds of different birds. Trees make safe homes for woodland birds. They build their nests high up among the leaves or hidden inside hollow trunks. A good place to wait for birds is near a clearing, where you can spot them coming out to feed on insects and seeds.

The treecreeper has a curved beak for picking insects out of cracks in the bark.

The treecreeper uses its stiff tail as a prop for hopping up tree trunks.

Tree climber

The treecreeper travels up and around tree trunks looking for food. It usually climbs upward only. When it reaches the top, it flies to the bottom of the next tree and starts all over again.

Forgotten trees

In autumn, look for jays collecting acorns. They bury them in the ground to eat later. But the birds forget many of the hiding places, and in spring the acorns sprout into little oak trees.

Acorns away

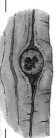

The acorn woodpecker wedges acorns firmly into the bark of a favorite tree to make a winter food supply.

Woodpecker warning

You might hear this woodpecker before you see it! With its powerful bill, it drums loudly on dead wood to proclaim its territory. Woodpeckers also use their bills to make nest holes in trees and to drill into rotten tree trunks in search of grubs (insect larvae) to eat.

The hairy woodpecker sits on its tail when it feeds its young.

Hidden in the leaves

The nightjar comes out at night to feed on moths. By day, it sits perfectly still on the rough ground. Its feathers match the dead leaves so well that it is almost impossible to spot the bird.

Desert and grassland birds

If you walk through the hot, dry desert or grassland at midday, you may not see many birds. Most seek shelter or shade from the sun's heat during the hottest part of the day. A few even feed at night. During the daytime, watch for large birds high in the sky and for flocks of small birds flitting around in search of seeds and insects. Water holes are good places to see desert birds, especially at sunrise and sunset.

Full speed ahead
The roadrunner runs across the desert chasing lizards and snakes. It can reach speeds of 12 miles per hour. When in danger, it prefers to run rather than fly.

The sand grouse is difficult to spot – its mottled sandy colors blend with the desert floor.

Thirsty chicks
Sand grouse often fly as far as 18 miles across the desert to find water. They have special breast feathers that soak up large amounts of water. The male sand grouse soaks his feathers in a pool or water hole, and then flies home. The thirsty chicks suck the water from his feathers.

Snake stalker

The secretary bird builds a nest of twigs
and dead branches on the top of a thorn
tree. This long-legged bird of prey stalks
the grassland in search of snakes
to eat, and then bites off their
heads before taking them
home to feed to its chicks.

*The ostrich
is the world's
fastest two-legged
runner. It can run
at up to 43 miles
per hour.*

Big bird

Ostriches wander across dry
grasslands in search of food and
water. They are the largest birds
in the world. Some stand over
eight feet tall – that's much
taller than a man!

*Ostriches are too big to fly,
but their long legs carry
them away from danger.*

Tropical birds

You will see some of the world's most colorful, spectacular birds in tropical forests. Parrots and toucans live in the treetops, and male birds of paradise display their beautiful feathers in special trees to attract mates. Jungle fowl and pheasants roam the forest floor, while eagles soar high overhead. Hummingbirds hover at flowers, and songbirds sing in their territories.

The toucan uses its huge beak to reach fruit hanging from small twigs.

What toucan do!

Toucans fly around the more open areas of tropical forests, calling out to one another with loud, frog-like croaks. They nest in small tree holes and may use the same site the following year.

On the lookout

These sulphur-crested cockatoos are on guard duty. They stay up in the trees while the rest of the flock eats seeds on the ground. If there is any sign of danger, the "guards" will shriek a loud warning.

With few enemies in the treetops, parrots do not have to camouflage their bright colors.

The long tail helps the parrot to balance as it twists and turns between the trees.

Brilliant colors

There are lots of parrots in tropical forests. They use their strong hooked beaks to crack seeds. Their beaks can also be a useful aid for climbing around in trees. Parrots usually fly in small groups. Listen for their harsh cries and look for their brilliant colors as they fly overhead.

You can recognize the male jungle fowl by the large red "comb" on his head.

Tropical chickens

The red jungle fowl is the domestic chicken's wild ancestor. Like chickens, jungle fowl live on the ground, where they scrape around for seeds. Can you hear them scuffling in the forest?

The female jungle fowl has dull colors to hide her while she sits on her eggs on the forest floor.

City birds

Many birds – starlings, sparrows, pigeons, even sea gulls – have learned to live with people. Small birds such as robins, tits, finches, and thrushes nest in hidden corners of city gardens, and owls take over empty buildings. In winter, watch for unusual visitors moving in from the country to feed on berries, rotting apples, and birdseed.

Messy birds

City pigeons roost and nest on the ledges of buildings. Their droppings mess up city streets and statues and are expensive to clean up.

Summer visitors

House martins build their mud nests under the eaves of city roofs. You can often spot their little white faces peering out. House martins are summer visitors, arriving in late April. After they have reared their young, they return to Africa in late September.

The house martin makes its nest out of mud. It uses sticky, wet mud to glue the nest into position.

Sooty swift

Luckily, the chimney swift is black! In the wild it nests in hollow trees, but in cities it chooses the next best thing – chimneys. It swoops down to sleep in unused factory chimneys. In the morning, it comes out a little dusty for the experience.

Look for the white crescent on a magpie's back as it flies.

City scavengers

Magpies feed on almost anything, including scraps of food dropped on the street and the eggs and young of smaller birds. Pigeons and thrushes often attack magpies to keep them away from their nests.

Mischievous magpies

Magpies are famous thieves. They like bright, shiny objects and will carry them off to decorate their nests. Magpies may even enter bedrooms to steal jewelry.

Index

A

acorn, 37, 52, 53
America, 44
anvil, 36
Archaeopteryx, 11
Arctic, 44
Auk, Little, 27
avocet, 48

Blue tit

B

bathing, 35
beak, 10, 11
bird of paradise, 21, 56
birds of prey, 11, 38
bird-watching, 8-9
bounding flight, 18, 19
breastbone, 11
buzzard, 13

C

cassowary, 22
chaffinch, 26-27, 30, 36
chickadee, black-capped, 36
chicken, 57
cockatoo, sulphur-crested, 56
cock-of-the-rock, 42
cormorant, 13
courtship, 20-21
crossbill, red, 37
cuckoo, 22, 28
curlew, 22
cygnets, 29

D

dabbling, 10
display, 42, 43
duck, 10, 16;
    mallard, 17, 50;
    wood, 27
ducklings, 23, 24, 27

E

eagle, 22, 56;
    bald, 38;
    martial, 18
eggtooth, 23

F

falcon, peregrine, 18
feathers, 12-13;
    cleaning, 34-35
finch, 58
flightless birds, 22, 55
fossil, 11
fowl, jungle, 56, 57;
    mallee, 32
frigate bird, 20-21, 47
fulmar, 16

Turnstone

G

gannet, 43, 46
godwit, bar-tailed, 48
goose, snow, 44-45
goshawk, 10
greenfinch, 10
guillemot, 22, 47
gull, 58;
    herring, 29, 49

H

hatching, 23
heron, 36;
    black, 36
hovering, 17, 19, 39
hummingbird, 12, 19, 22, 56

Mallard

IJK

incubation, 22

jay, 52

keel, 11
kestrel, 12-13, 17, 39
kingfisher, 50, 51

MN

magpie, 31, 59
martin, house, 58
migration, 44-45
muscles, 11, 17

nest building, 30-33
nestlings, 24-25
nightjar, 53
nuthatch, 37

O

ostrich, 55
owl, 13, 14-15, 40-41, 58;
    barn, 14-15, 41;
    long-eared, 40
oystercatcher, 49

P

parent birds, 28-29
parrot, 56, 57
pelican, 29
pellets, owl, 41
penguin, 28
perching birds, 11
pheasant, 56
pigeon, 14, 15, 58, 59
plumage, 42
preen gland, 34
puffin, 46, 47

RS

redstart, 22
roadrunner, 54

Kingfisher

robin, 58;
    American, 22;
    European, 43
roost, 58

sand grouse, 54
seabirds, 46-47
secretary bird, 55
shells, 36, 49
shrike, 38
soaring flight, 16, 18, 39
songbirds, 56
sparrow, 58;
    house, 8
spoonbill, 51
starling, 10-11, 34, 35, 36, 58
stoop, 18
swallow, 45;

cliff, 33
swan, 12, 29
swift, 36;
    chimney, 59
swiftlet, cave, 32

Oystercatcher

T

tern, Arctic, 44;
    Sandwich, 20
territory, 42-43, 53
thrush, song, 31, 36, 58, 59
tit, 36, 37, 58;
    blue, 19, 24-25;
    penduline, 33
toucan, 56
treecreeper, 52
turnstone, 49

V

vision, 40
vulture, 39;
    king, 39

Egg hatching

W

waders, 48-49
warbler, reed, 33
weaver bird, 32
webbed feet, 11, 47
woodpecker, acorn, 53;
    hairy, 53

Acknowledgments

**Dorling Kindersley
would like to thank:**
Simon Battensby for
photography on pages 11
and 12.
Sharon Grant for design
assistance.
Gin von Noorden and Kate
Raworth for editorial
assistance and research.
Jane Parker for the index.
Kim Taylor for special
photography on pages 14-15,
23, 24-25, 26-27, 52.

Illustrations by:
Diana Catchpole, Angelika
Elsebach, Jane Gedye, Nick
Hewetson, Ruth Lindsay,
Louis Mackay, Polly Noakes,
Lorna Turpin.

Picture credits
t=top b=bottom c=center
l=left r=right
Frank Blackburn: 41bl, 58b.
Bruce Coleman Ltd: 53cl,
55b; /J. & D. Bartlett 28b; /
Jane Burton 57bl; /Jeff Foott
38l; /Hans Reinhard 40t, 42l;
/Kim Taylor 34; /Roger
Wilmshurst 36br.
Frank Lane Picture Agency:
19t, 49b; /Philip Berry 18c; /
W.S. Clark 50b; /Peggy
Heard 35t; /R. van Nostrand
20b, 21b; /P. Perry 29tr; /J.
Watkins 46-7; /R.
Wilmshurst 43b, 51tr.
Natural History
Photographic Agency: /
Michael Leach 45b; /Harold
Palo 39br.
Bill Coster 16.
Peter Chadwick 37bl.
Cyril Laubscher 48, 57.
Roger Steele 18.
Kim Taylor 8, 10, 37br.